AMERICAN
ORIGINAL
MONTAUK
MONTAUK
INDIAN

NANTUCKET ISLAND

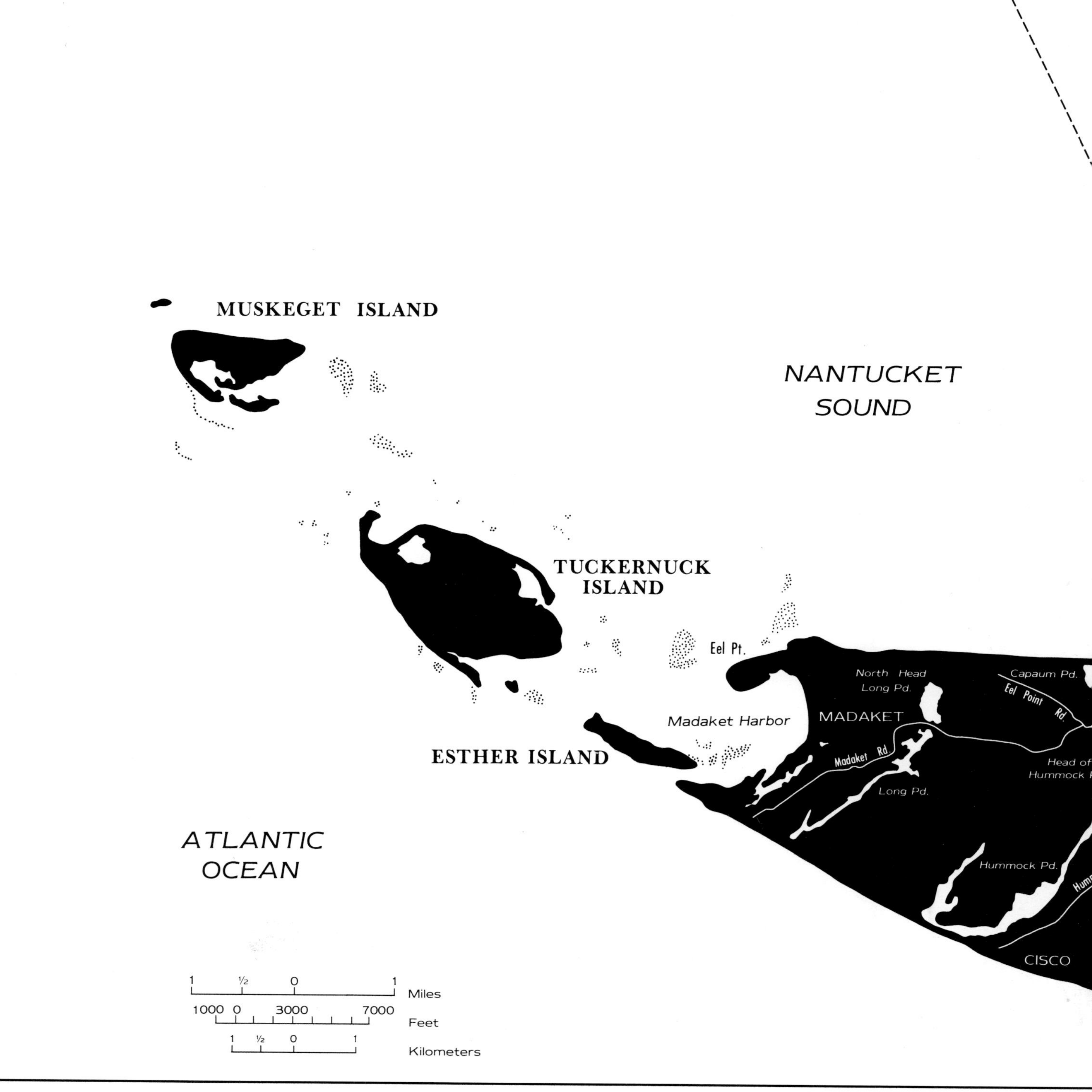

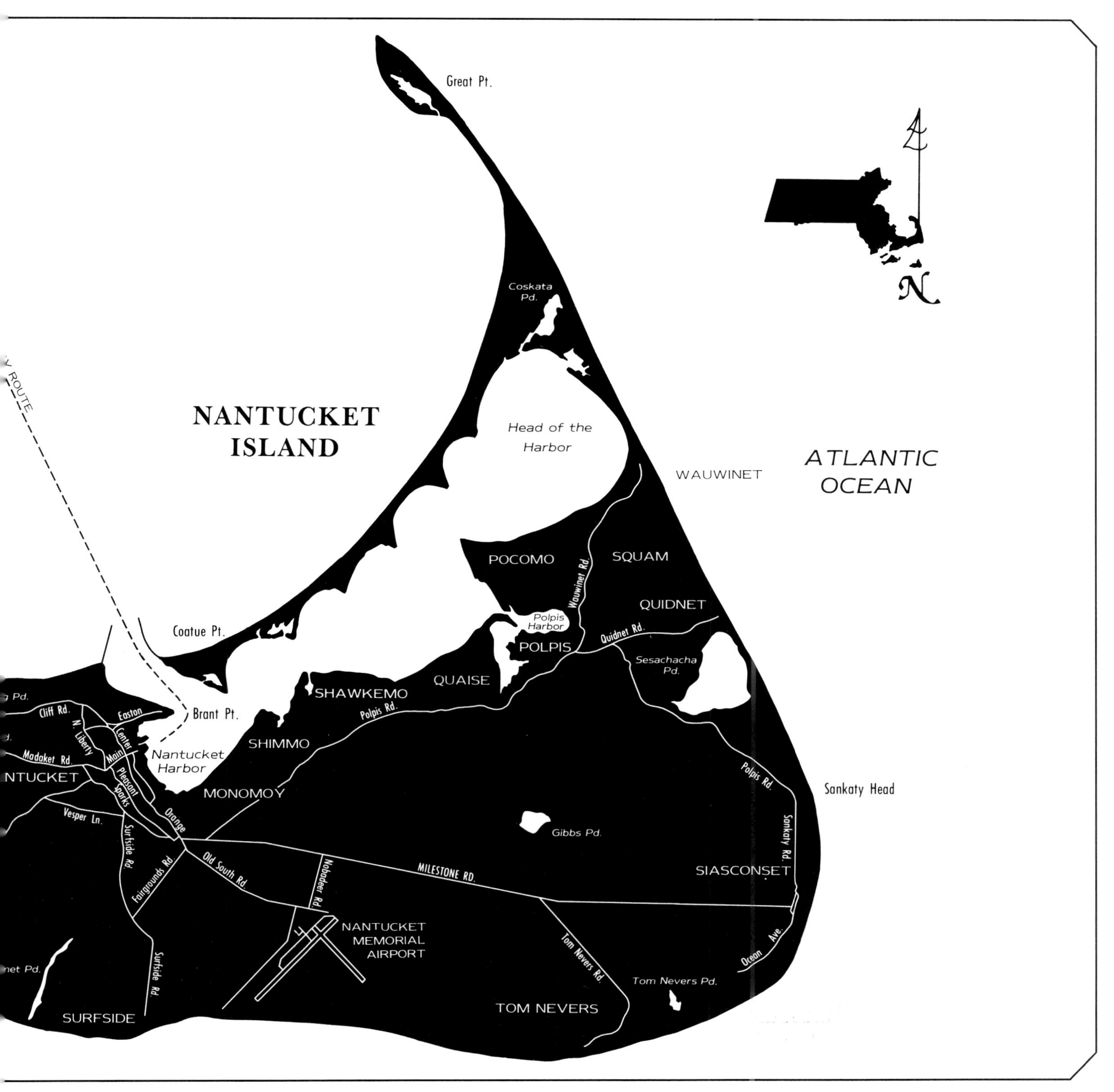

Great Pt.
NANTUCKET ISLAND
ATLANTIC OCEAN
Coskata Pd.
Head of the Harbor
WAUWINET
POCOMO
SQUAM
Wauwinet Rd.
QUIDNET
Polpis Harbor
POLPIS
Quidnet Rd.
Coatue Pt.
Sesachacha Pd.
QUAISE
SHAWKEMO
Polpis Rd.
Brant Pt.
Cliff Rd.
Easton
Center
Polpis Rd.
N. Liberty
SHIMMO
Madaket Rd.
Main
Nantucket Harbor
Sankaty Head
Pd.
NTUCKET
Pleasant
Sparks
MONOMOY
Vesper Ln.
Orange
Gibbs Pd.
Surfside Rd.
Fairgrounds Rd.
Old South Rd.
MILESTONE RD.
SIASCONSET
Nobadeer Rd.
Sankaty Rd.
net Pd.
Surfside Rd.
NANTUCKET MEMORIAL AIRPORT
Tom Nevers Rd.
Ocean Ave.
SURFSIDE
Tom Nevers Pd.
TOM NEVERS
Y ROUTE
N

Rejected Works Publishing House, Ltd.
2633 Riverside Dr.
Columbus, IN 47201

Printed in the United States of America by Heath Printers, Seattle, Washington

Library of Congress Catalog Card Number: 84-62252

ISBN 0-932493-00-9 (pbk.)

Sweet Dreams Nantucket
Images of Nantucket Island

Designed & Photographed by Tom Simms
Maps by Rebecca Brown

Rejected Works Publishing House, Ltd.

Sweet Dreams Nantucket

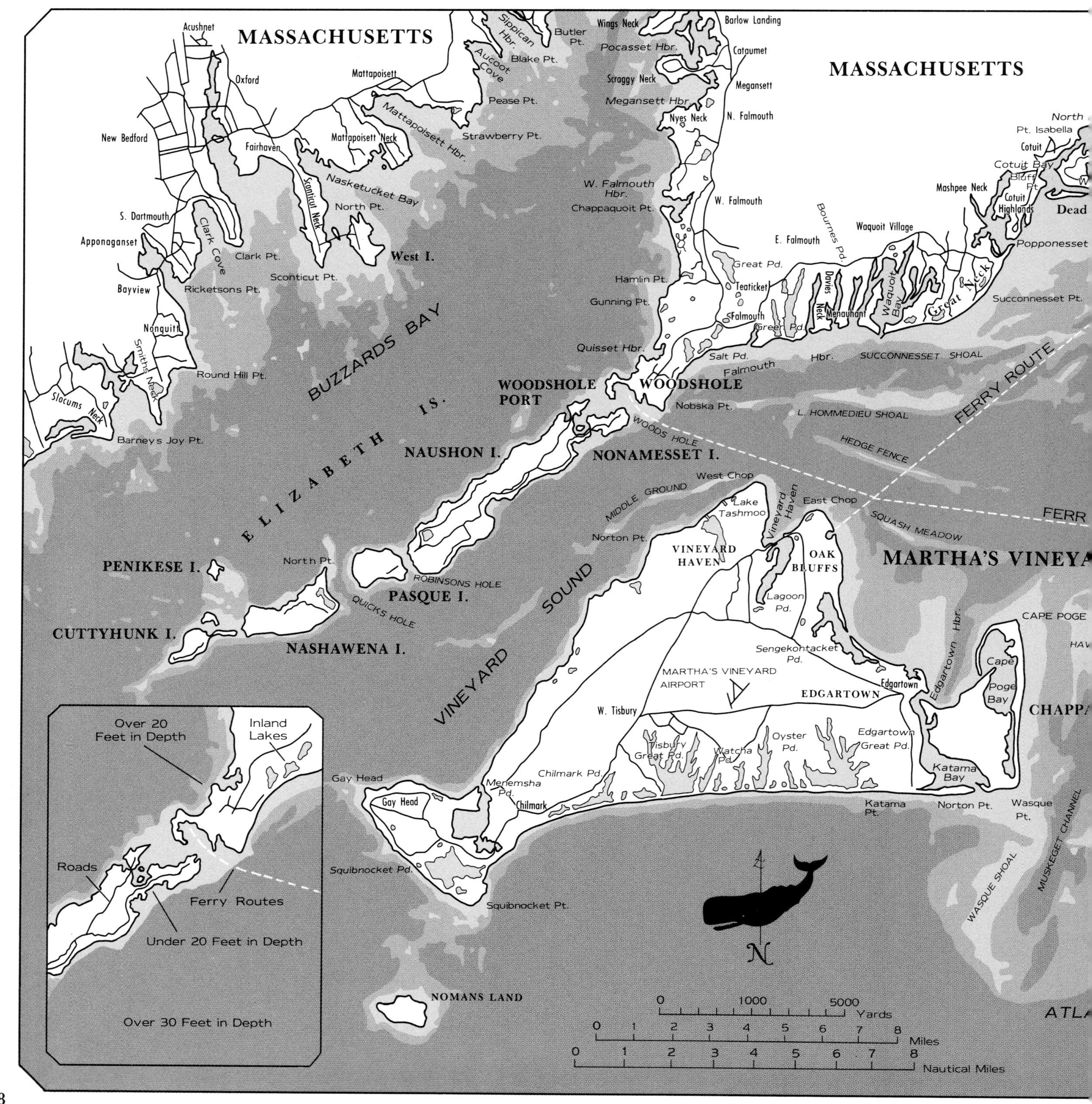

MASSACHUSETTS
MASSACHUSETTS
Acushnet
Oxford
Mattapoisett
Sippican Hbr.
Butler Pt.
Wings Neck
Barlow Landing
Pocasset Hbr.
Cataumet
Aucoot Cove
Blake Pt.
Scraggy Neck
Megansett
New Bedford
Mattapoisett
Pease Pt.
Megansett Hbr.
N. Falmouth
Fairhaven
Mattapoisett Neck
Strawberry Pt.
Nyes Neck
North
Pt. Isabella
Cotuit
Mattapoisett Hbr.
Cotuit Bay
Bluff Pt.
Mashpee Neck
S. Dartmouth
North Pt.
W. Falmouth Hbr.
Cotuit Highlands
Nasketucket Bay
Chappaquoit Pt.
W. Falmouth
Dead
Apponaganset
Clark Cove
Scotnicut Neck
Waquoit Village
Popponesset
Bayview
Clark Pt.
West I.
E. Falmouth
Bournes Pd.
Ricketsons Pt.
Sconticut Pt.
Hamlin Pt.
Great Pd.
Davies Neck
Waquoit Bay
Great Neck
Succonnesset Pt.
Nonquitt
Teaticket
Gunning Pt.
Menauhant
Smiths Neck
Quisset Hbr.
Falmouth
Green Pd.
Round Hill Pt.
Salt Pd.
SUCCONNESSET SHOAL
BUZZARDS BAY
Falmouth Hbr.
FERRY ROUTE
Slocums Neck
WOODSHOLE PORT
WOODSHOLE
Barneys Joy Pt.
Nobska Pt.
L. HOMMEDIEU SHOAL
ELIZABETH IS.
WOODS HOLE
HEDGE FENCE
NAUSHON I.
NONAMESSET I.
West Chop
Vineyard Haven
East Chop
FERRY
MIDDLE GROUND
Lake Tashmoo
SQUASH MEADOW
PENIKESE I.
North Pt.
Norton Pt.
VINEYARD HAVEN
OAK BLUFFS
MARTHA'S VINEYARD
ROBINSONS HOLE
SOUND
Lagoon Pd.
PASQUE I.
CAPE POGE
QUICKS HOLE
Sengekontacket Pd.
HAW
CUTTYHUNK I.
MARTHA'S VINEYARD AIRPORT
Edgartown
Cape Poge Bay
NASHAWENA I.
EDGARTOWN
Edgartown Hbr.
VINEYARD
W. Tisbury
CHAPPA
Oyster Pd.
Edgartown Great Pd.
Over 20 Feet in Depth
Inland Lakes
Tisbury Great Pd.
Watcha Pd.
Katama Bay
Gay Head
Chilmark Pd.
Menemsha Pd.
Katama Pt.
Norton Pt.
Wasque Pt.
Gay Head
Chilmark
Katama
Roads
Ferry Routes
N
WASQUE SHOAL
MUSKEGET CHANNEL
Under 20 Feet in Depth
Squibnocket Pd.
Squibnocket Pt.
Over 30 Feet in Depth
NOMANS LAND
ATLA
0   1000   5000
Yards
0   1   2   3   4   5   6   7   8
Miles
0   1   2   3   4   5   6   7   8
Nautical Miles

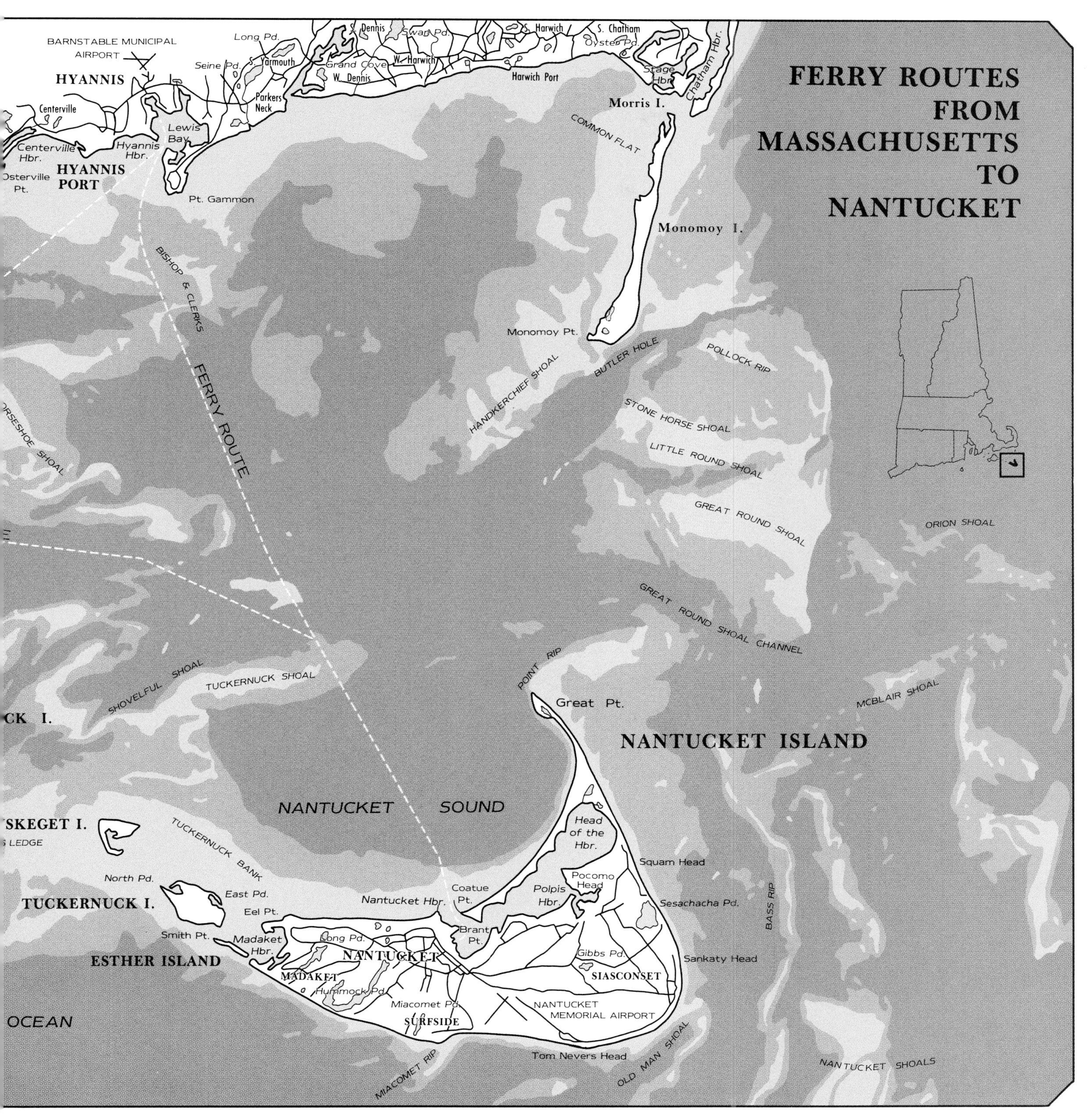
FERRY ROUTES FROM MASSACHUSETTS TO NANTUCKET
BARNSTABLE MUNICIPAL AIRPORT
HYANNIS
Centerville
Centerville Hbr.
HYANNIS PORT
Osterville Pt.
Lewis Bay
Hyannis Hbr.
Pt. Gammon
Long Pd.
Seine Pd.
S. Yarmouth
Parkers Neck
Grand Cove
W. Dennis
S. Dennis
Swan Pd.
W. Harwich
Harwich Port
S. Harwich
S. Chatham
Oyster Pd.
Stage Hbr.
Chatham Hbr.
Morris I.
COMMON FLAT
Monomoy I.
Monomoy Pt.
BUTLER HOLE
HANDKERCHIEF SHOAL
POLLOCK RIP
STONE HORSE SHOAL
LITTLE ROUND SHOAL
GREAT ROUND SHOAL
ORION SHOAL
BISHOP & CLERKS
FERRY ROUTE
HORSESHOE SHOAL
GREAT ROUND SHOAL CHANNEL
SHOVELFUL SHOAL
TUCKERNUCK SHOAL
POINT RIP
MCBLAIR SHOAL
Great Pt.
NANTUCKET ISLAND
CK I.
SKEGET I.
LEDGE
NANTUCKET SOUND
TUCKERNUCK BANK
Head of the Hbr.
Squam Head
Pocomo Head
Polpis Hbr.
Sesachacha Pd.
BASS RIP
North Pd.
East Pd.
Eel Pt.
Coatue Pt.
Nantucket Hbr.
TUCKERNUCK I.
Smith Pt.
Madaket Hbr.
Long Pd.
Brant Pt.
ESTHER ISLAND
MADAKET
NANTUCKET
Hummock Pd.
Gibbs Pd.
Sankaty Head
SIASCONSET
Miacomet Pd.
NANTUCKET MEMORIAL AIRPORT
SURFSIDE
MIACOMET RIP
Tom Nevers Head
OLD MAN SHOAL
NANTUCKET SHOALS
OCEAN

Boarding Steamship at Hyannis Port, Massachusetts...

Leaving Lewis Bay...

Nantucket— 2½ hrs away...

halfway...

distance...
Nantucket in

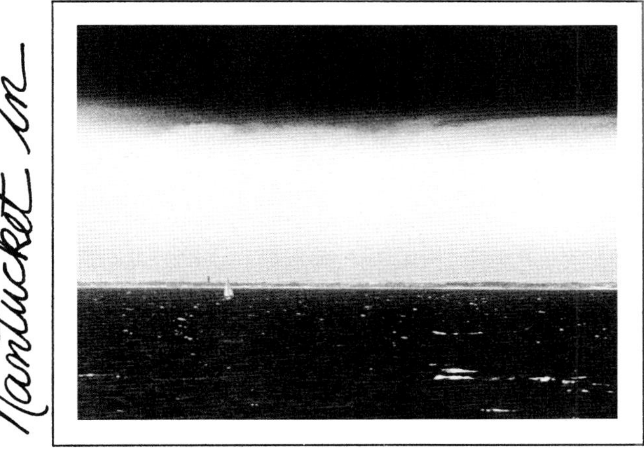

Coming into Nantucket Harbor...

Nantucket, Nantucket, Nantucket, Nantucket ...

PORTOBELLO

Nantucket

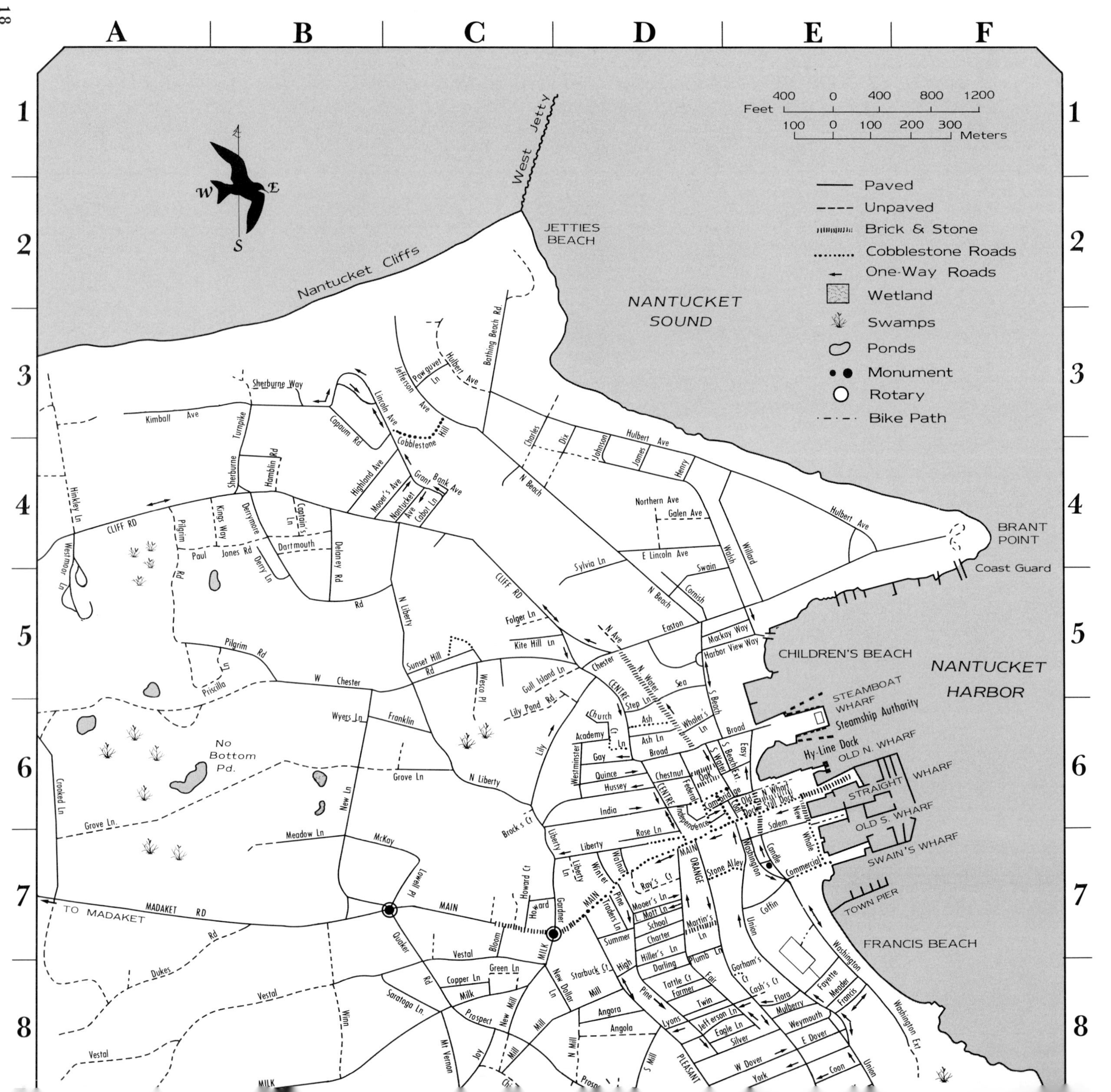

A   B   C   D   E   F
Feet   400   0   400   800   1200
100   0   100   200   300   Meters
Paved
Unpaved
Brick & Stone
Cobblestone Roads
One-Way Roads
Wetland
Swamps
Ponds
Monument
Rotary
Bike Path
West Jetty
JETTIES BEACH
Nantucket Cliffs
NANTUCKET SOUND
NANTUCKET HARBOR
CHILDREN'S BEACH
FRANCIS BEACH
BRANT POINT
Coast Guard
STEAMBOAT WHARF
Steamship Authority
Hy-Line Dock
OLD N. WHARF
STRAIGHT WHARF
OLD S. WHARF
SWAIN'S WHARF
TOWN PIER
Old N. Wharf
Hy-Line Dock
New
Whale
Salem
Candle
Commercial
Stone Alley
Washington
Union
Coffin
Sherburne Way
Kimball Ave
Turnpike
Capaum Rd
Jefferson
Pawguvet Ln
Hulbert Ave
Bathing Beach Rd.
Lincoln Ave
Cobblestone Hill
Highland Ave
Mooer's Ave
Nantucket Ave
Cabot Ln
Grant
Bank Ave
Charles
Dix
Johnson
James
Henry
Hulbert Ave
N Beach
Northern Ave
Galen Ave
E Lincoln Ave
Sylvia Ln
Swain
Cornish
Walsh
Willard
Hulbert Ave
Sherburne
Hamblin Rd
Kings Way
Derrymore
Captain's Ln
Dartmouth
Delaney Rd
Hinkley Ln
Westmoor Ln
CLIFF RD
Pilgrim Rd
Paul
Jones Rd
Derry Ln
Rd
N Liberty
CLIFF RD
N Beach
Easton
Mackay Way
Harbor View Way
Folger Ln
Kite Hill Ln
N Ave
N Water
Sea
S Beach
Chester
CENTRE
Step Ln
Whaler's Ln
Broad
Easy
S Beach Ext.
S Water
Pilgrim Rd
Priscilla
Sunset Hill Rd
Wesco Pl
Gull Island Ln
Lily Pond Rd
Lily
W Chester
Wyers Ln
Franklin
Grove Ln
N Liberty
No Bottom Pd.
Crooked Ln
Grove Ln
New Ln
Meadow Ln
McKay
Lowell Pl
TO MADAKET
MADAKET RD
Rd
Dukes
Vestal
Saratoga Ln
Winn
Vestal
Church
Academy
Westminster
Gay
Quince
Hussey
India
Ash
Ash Ln
Broad
Chestnut
Federal
CENTRE
Independence
Rose Ln
Liberty
Liberty
Liberty Ln
Brock's Ct
Walnut
Winter
Pine
Traders Ln
Mooer's Ln
Mott Ln
School
Charter
Hiller's Ln
Darling
Tattle Ct
Farmer
Ray's Ct
Howard Ct
Howard
Gardner
MAIN
MAIN
ORANGE
Martin's Ln
Summer
High
Starbuck Ct
Mill
Pine
Angora
Angola
Lyons
Jefferson Ln
Eagle Ln
Silver
Twin
Fair
Plumb
Gorham's Ct
Cash's Ct
Flora
Mulberry
Weymouth
E Dover
W Dover
York
Coon
Fayette
Madder
Francis
Coffin
Union
Washington
Washington Ext
Bloom
Milk
New Dollar Ln
Quaker
Vestal
Copper Ln
Green Ln
Milk
New Mill
Prospect
Mt Vernon
Joy
Mill
N Mill
S Mill
PLEASANT
Prospect
MILK
W Dover
York
Stone Alley

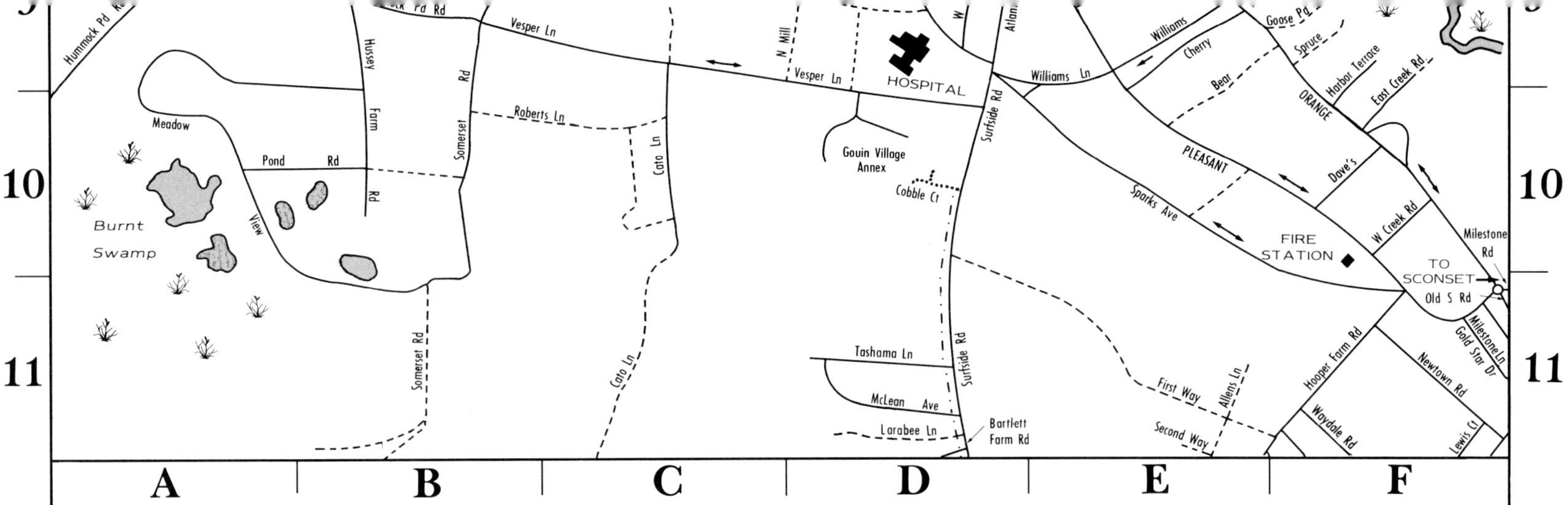

Hummock Rd Rd
Vesper Ln
N. Mill
Williams
Cherry
Goose Pd
Spruce
Harbor Terrace
East Creek Rd
Meadow
Hussey
Farm
Rd
Roberts Ln
Vesper Ln
HOSPITAL
Surfside Rd
Williams Ln
Bear
ORANGE
Pond Rd
Somerset
View
Cato Ln
Gouin Village Annex
Cobble Ct
PLEASANT
Dave's
Sparks Ave
W. Creek Rd
Burnt Swamp
FIRE STATION
Milestone Rd
TO SCONSET
Old S Rd
Milestone Ln
Gold Star Dr
Tashama Ln
Surfside Rd
McLean Ave
Larabee Ln
Bartlett Farm Rd
First Way
Allens Ln
Second Way
Hooper Farm Rd
Newtown Rd
Waydale Rd
Lewis Ct
Somerset Rd
Pond Rd
A   B   C   D   E   F
10   11

Information Centre

25 Federal Street

Bikes, Bikes, Bikes, Bikes, Bikes, Bikes, Bikes, Bikes,

Bikes, Bikes, Rent, Rent, Rent, no cars if you can,

please, please.

Please ...

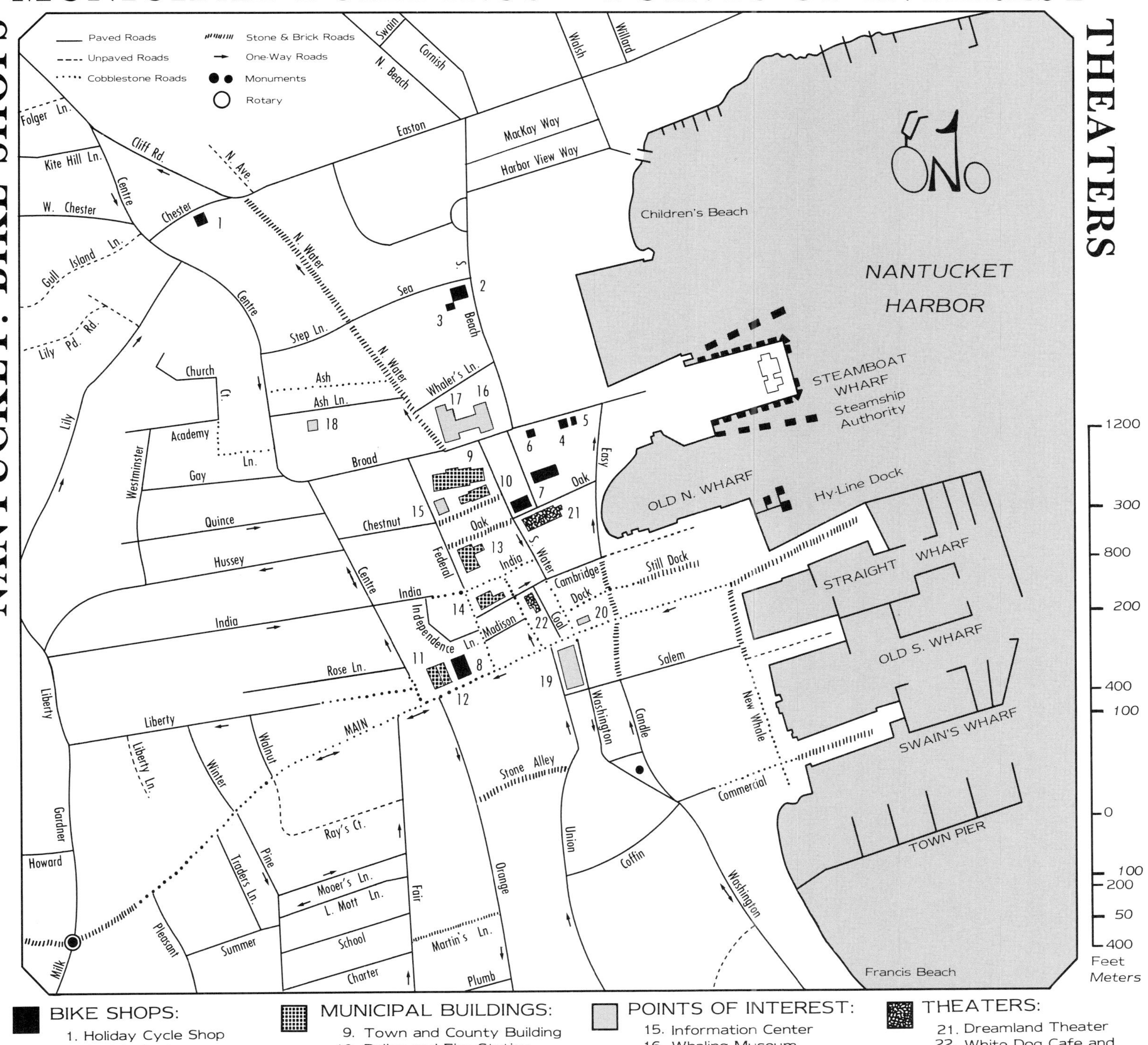

BIKE SHOPS:
1. Holiday Cycle Shop
2. Cook's Cycles
3. Sprockets
4. Young's Bike Shop
5. Nantucket Bike Shop
6. Nantucket Bike Shop II
7. Nantucket Moped and Rentals
8. Snow's Cycle

MUNICIPAL BUILDINGS:
9. Town and County Building
10. Police and Fire Station
11. Congdon's Pharmacy
12. Nantucket Pharmacy
13. Atheneum (Library)
14. Post Office

POINTS OF INTEREST:
15. Information Center
16. Whaling Museum
17. Peter Foulger Museum
18. Nantucket Accomodations
19. Nantucket Historical Association
20. Nantucket Chamber of Commerce (In the Pacific Club Building)

THEATERS:
21. Dreamland Theater
22. White Dog Cafe and Theater

23

Inns, Hotels & Cottages

Section I

Jared Coffin House

29 Broad Street

open year 'round

Guest House
The Four Chimneys

38 Orange Street

The White Elephant

Swain's Wharf

Wharf Cottages

Easton Street

The Summer House

Cottage

Inn &

Ocean Avenue, Siasconset

NANTUCKET: INNS
BRANT PT.
Cliff Rd.
Hinkley Ln.
Pilgrim Rd.
Kings Way
Paul Jones Rd.
Westmoor Ln.
79
Pl.
Delany
Rd.
Derrymore Rd.
1
N. Liberty
N. Beach
(See Inset)
80
Dix
James
Johnson
Henry
Hulbert Ave.
Northern Ave.
Galen Ave.
Welsh
Willard
E. Lincoln Ave.
5
2
4
3
Sylvia Ave.
N. Beach
Cornish Ct.
Swain
Cornish
Easton
Cliff Rd.
11
12
13
15
Folger Ln.
8
10
Easton
Mackay Way
14
Kite Hill Ln.
9
16
W. Chester
7
Chester
17
Harbor View Way
Centre
N. Water
18
Children's Beach
Sunset Hill Rd.
6
27
21
22
W. Chester
28
26
19
Sea
STEAMBOAT WHARF
Gull Island Ln.
Centre
23
20
29
25
24
S. Beach
Wesco Pl.
30
34
Steamship Authority
Wyers Ln.
Franklin
Lily Pd. Rd.
31
32
33
35
Church
Ash Ln.
Whaler's Ln.
Lily
Ash
Broad
S. Beach
Easy
Academy
36
39
41
OLD N. WHARF
Grove Ln.
Grove Ln.
37
38
40
Hy-Line Dock
N. Liberty
Gay
43
45
48
Chestnut
S. Water
Oak
STRAIGHT WHARF
Westminster
42
Quince
44
47
46
Oak
55
New Lane
Hussey
52
Federal
Old N. Wharf
Meadow Ln.
McKay
51
53
Cambridge
Dock
Still Dock
62
OLD S. WHARF
49
54
Coal
Center
India
50
Independence
Salem
New Whale
SWAIN'S WHARF
Liberty
Rose Ln.
MAIN
Lowell Pl.
Liberty
60
68
Liberty Ln.
TOWN PIER
MADAKET RD.
MAIN
56
Commercial
To Madaket
Walnut Ln.
57
59
Candle
Winter
Stone Alley
61
NANTUCKET
Howard Ct.
58
Ray's Ct.
Coffin
HARBOR
63
Gardner
MAIN
64
Mooer's Ln.
65
67
Quaker Rd.
Howard
Traders Ln.
L. Mott Ln.
Fair
Orange
Washington
Bloom
Summer
66
Francis Beach
Milk
Pleasant
School
Martin's Ln.
Vestal
Pine
Charter
Plumb Ln.
Fayette
Meader
Starbuck Ct.
69
71
72
Union
Francis
Green Ln.
High
Hiller's Ln.
70
Cooper Ln.
New Dollar Ln.
Darling
Saratoga Ln.
Tattle Ct.
Cash's Ct.
Flora
Prospect
Farmer
Fair
Mulberry
Weymouth
Mt. Vernon
Angora
Pine
Twin
73
Milk
N. Mill
Lyons
Jefferson Ln.
74
E. Dover
Joy
Angola
Eagle Ln.
Silver
York
75
S. Mill
W. Dover
Coon
Beaver
Hummock Pd. Rd.
York
76
Union
Vesper Ln.
Warren
Spring
Farm Rd.
Meadow View Dr.
(See Inset)
Chicken Hill
New
Orange
Sommerset Rd.
Hussey
Prospect
York
Back
The Creeks
N. Mill
S. Prospect
W. York Ln.
Atlantic Ave.
Pleasant
To Sconset
Roberts Ln.
77
78
Pond Rd.
Pond Rd.
S. Prospect
Williams
Washington Ext.
N
Feet
400 50 0 400 800 1200
Meters
100 0 100 200 300

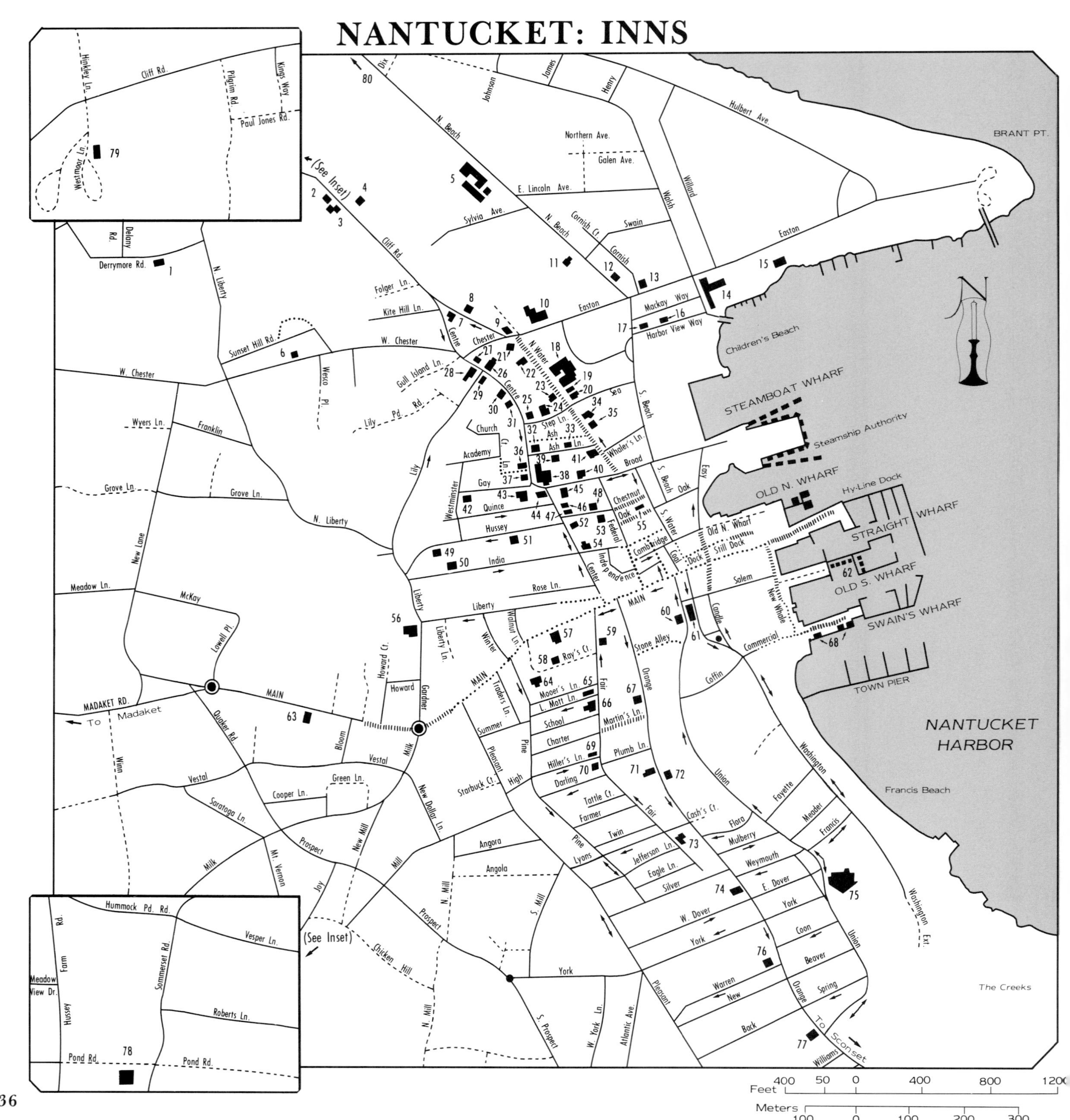

36

SIASCONSET: INNS

INNS: NANTUCKET

1. The Hungry Whale
2. The Cliff House
3. The House of Seven Gables
4. Fair Winds Guest House
5. Beachside Motel
6. 29 West Chester
7. The Century House
8. The Cliff Lodge
9. Captain's Corner
10. The Gordon Folger Hotel
11. Dolphin Guest Inn
12. Beachway Guests
13. Ledwell Guests
14. The White Elephant
15. The Breakers Inn
16. Nantucket Landfall
17. Safe Harbor Guest House
18. The Harbor House
19. Easton House
20. Hussey House
21. Ivy Lodge
22. Carlisle House
23. Island Reef
24. The Overlook
25. The Corner House
26. Martin's Guest House
27. The Centre Board
28. Holiday Inn
29. Captain Gardner House
30. Chatter Box
31. Anchor Inn
32. 1739 House
33. Four Ash Street
34. The Brass Lantern
35. The Periwinkle
36. The Jared Coffin House
37. The Jared Coffin House
38. The Jared Coffin House
39. Six Ash Lane
40. Nesbitt Inn
41. Nantucket Whaler
42. House at Ten Gay St.
43. While Away Guest House

44. The White House
45. Le Languedoc
46. Cranberry Guest House
47. Quaker House Inn
48. Chestnut House
49. The Gray Goose
50. India House
51. Ten Hussey Street
52. The Royal Manor
53. Hawthorne House
54. The Roberts House Inn
55. The Parker House
56. 18 Gardner St. Guest House
57. 76 Main Street
58. The Carriage House
59. Sixfair Guest House
60. Ayers Guest House
61. Ayers Guest House
62. Wharf Cottages
63. La Petite Maison
64. The Raycroft
65. The Barnacle Inn
66. The Ships Inn
67. House of Orange
68. Wharf Cottages
69. Fair Gardens
70. The Woodbox
71. Grieder Guest House
72. The Four Chimneys Inn
73. The Phillips House
74. 75 Orange Street
75. The Elegant Dump Dormitory
76. 95 Orange Street
77. The Stumble Inn
78. The Guest House
79. The Westmoor Inn
80. The Cliff Side Beach Club

INNS: SCONSET

81. Le Chanticleer
82. The Wade Guest Houses
83. The Summer House

Paved Roads
Unpaved Roads
Bike Path
One-way Roads
Inns

0   ½   1   Mile
0   1   2   Kilometers

47 Main Street

Congdon's Pharmacy

45 Main Street

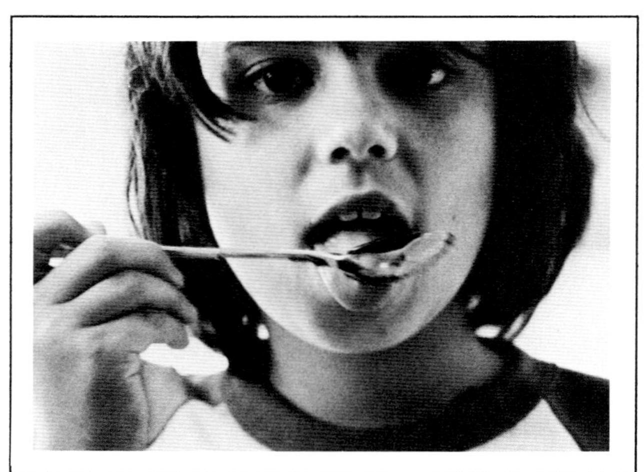

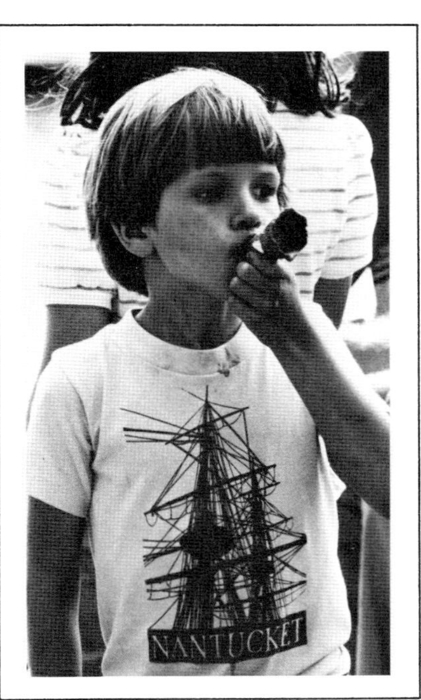

Restaurants, Restaurants, Restaurants

Section II

The Downy Flake Restaurant

South Water Street

Breakfast & Lunch

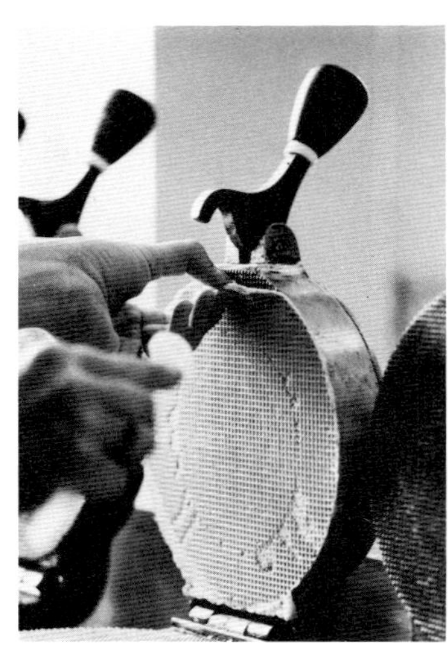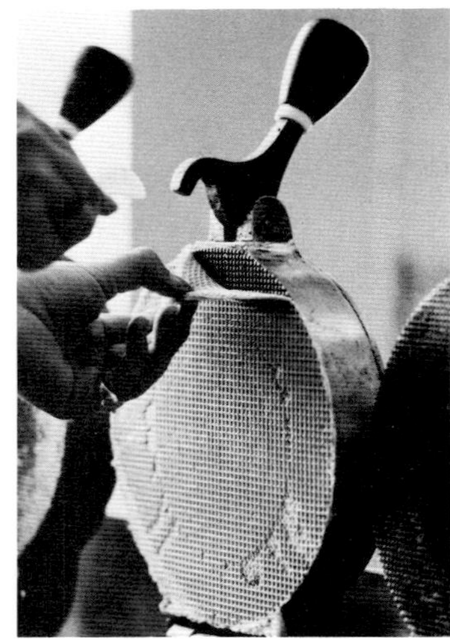

The Sweet Shop

40 Main Street

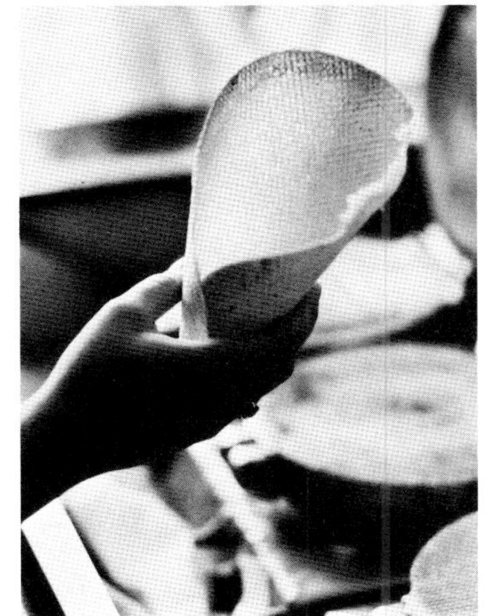

Lunch & Dinner & ice cream, ice cream.

The Skipper Restaurant

THE SKIPPER

Steamboat Wharf

Lunch & Dinner

The Atlantic Cafe

15 South Water Street

Lunch & Dinner

open year 'round

23 Broad St.

The Brotherhood of Thieves

open year 'round

Lunch & Dinner

The Whale at the Gordon Folger

THE WHALE
Good food and drink aplenty

Easton Street

Breakfast & Dinner

29 Broad Street

Dining at The Jared

Breakfast & Dinner

reservations for dinner

open year 'round

Reservations

The Woodbox

29 Fair Street

Breakfast & Dinner

D. Manco
9 India Street

reservations

Dinner

Company of the Cauldron

7 India Street

Dinner

Ocean Avenue, Siasconset

The Summer House Restaurant

reservations

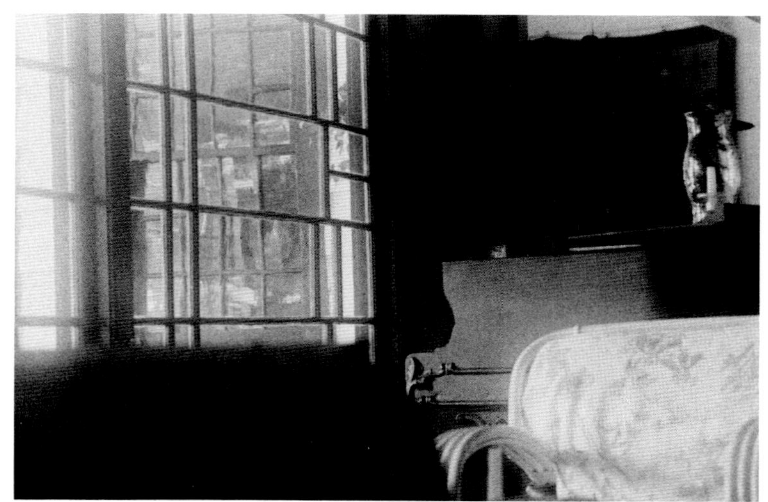

Lunch, Dinner & Sunday Brunch

Le Chanticleer

reservations

Lunch & Dinner

Siasconset

New Street,

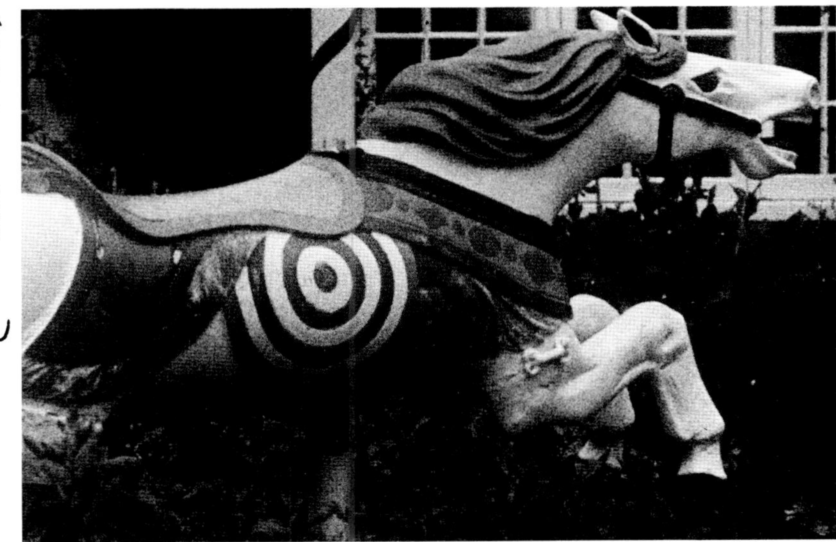

NANTUCKET: RESTAURANTS

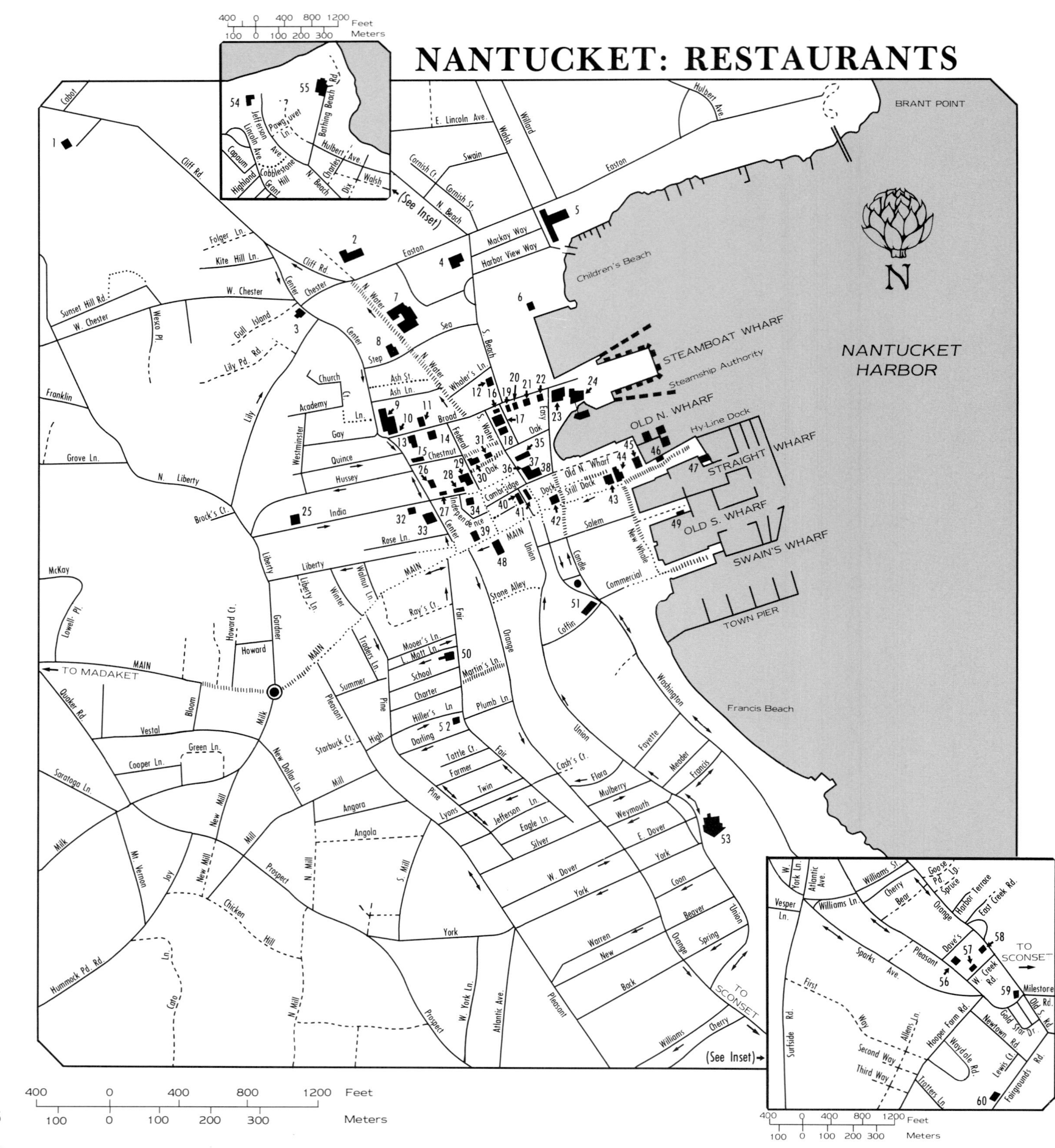

SIASCONSET: RESTAURANTS

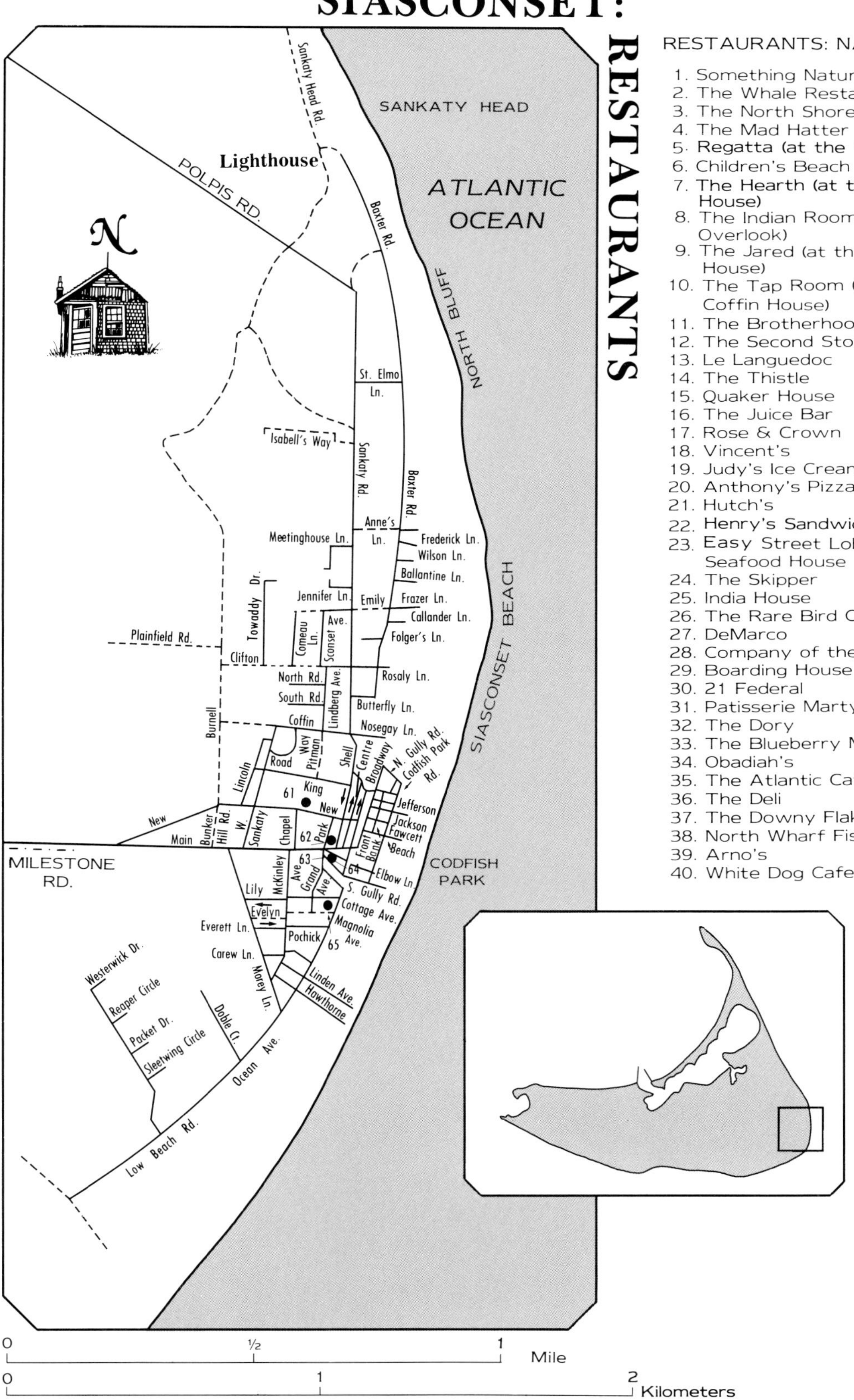

RESTAURANTS: NANTUCKET

1. Something Natural
2. The Whale Restaurant
3. The North Shore Restaurant
4. The Mad Hatter
5. Regatta (at the White Elephant)
6. Children's Beach Snack Bar
7. The Hearth (at the Harbor House)
8. The Indian Room (at the Overlook)
9. The Jared (at the Jared Coffin House)
10. The Tap Room (at the Jared Coffin House)
11. The Brotherhood of Thieves
12. The Second Story
13. Le Languedoc
14. The Thistle
15. Quaker House
16. The Juice Bar
17. Rose & Crown
18. Vincent's
19. Judy's Ice Cream
20. Anthony's Pizza
21. Hutch's
22. Henry's Sandwiches
23. Easy Street Lobster and Seafood House
24. The Skipper
25. India House
26. The Rare Bird Cafe
27. DeMarco
28. Company of the Cauldron
29. Boarding House
30. 21 Federal
31. Patisserie Marty
32. The Dory
33. The Blueberry Muffin
34. Obadiah's
35. The Atlantic Cafe
36. The Deli
37. The Downy Flake
38. North Wharf Fish House
39. Arno's
40. White Dog Cafe
41. The Opera House
42. The Club Car
43. Cap'n Tobey's Chowder House
44. The Tavern
45. Straight Wharf Restaurant
46. Nantucket Yogurt
47. The Water Club
48. The Sweet Shop
49. The Morning Glory Cafe
50. The Captain's Table
51. The Lobster Trap
52. The Woodbox
53. The Elegant Dump Diner
54. The Galley
55. Hutche's at Jettie's Beach
56. Jean's Restaurant
57. The Upper Crust
58. Food for Here & There
59. The Rotary
60. Christopher's

RESTAURANTS: SCONSET

61. Le Chanticleer
62. The Pourch
63. Claudette's Catering
64. Sconset Cafe
65. The Summer House

Nantucket Lightship Baskets

1772

Historical Sites

Section III

Fair Street

Friends Meeting House

Built 1846

Fair Street Museum

Summer St., & Traders Lane

Baptist Church

Built 1840

The Whaling Museum

Broad Street

The Three Bricks

East Brick

97 Main Street

95 Main Street

Built between 1836 & 1838

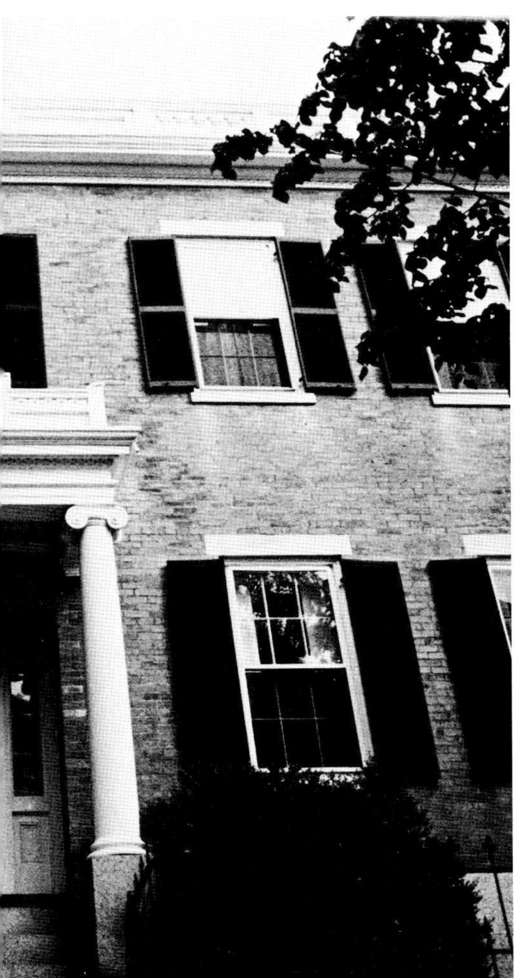

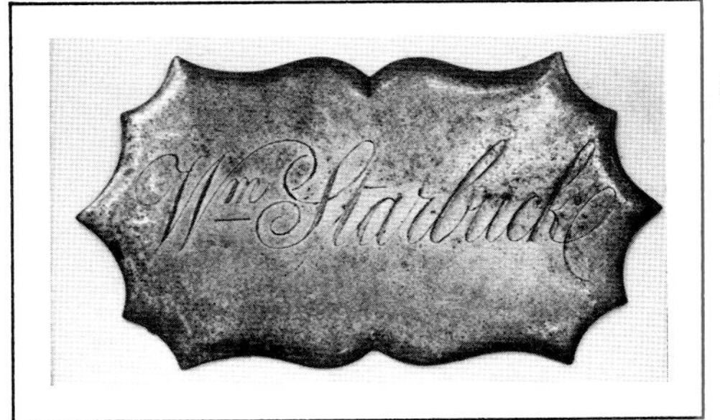

Middle Brick

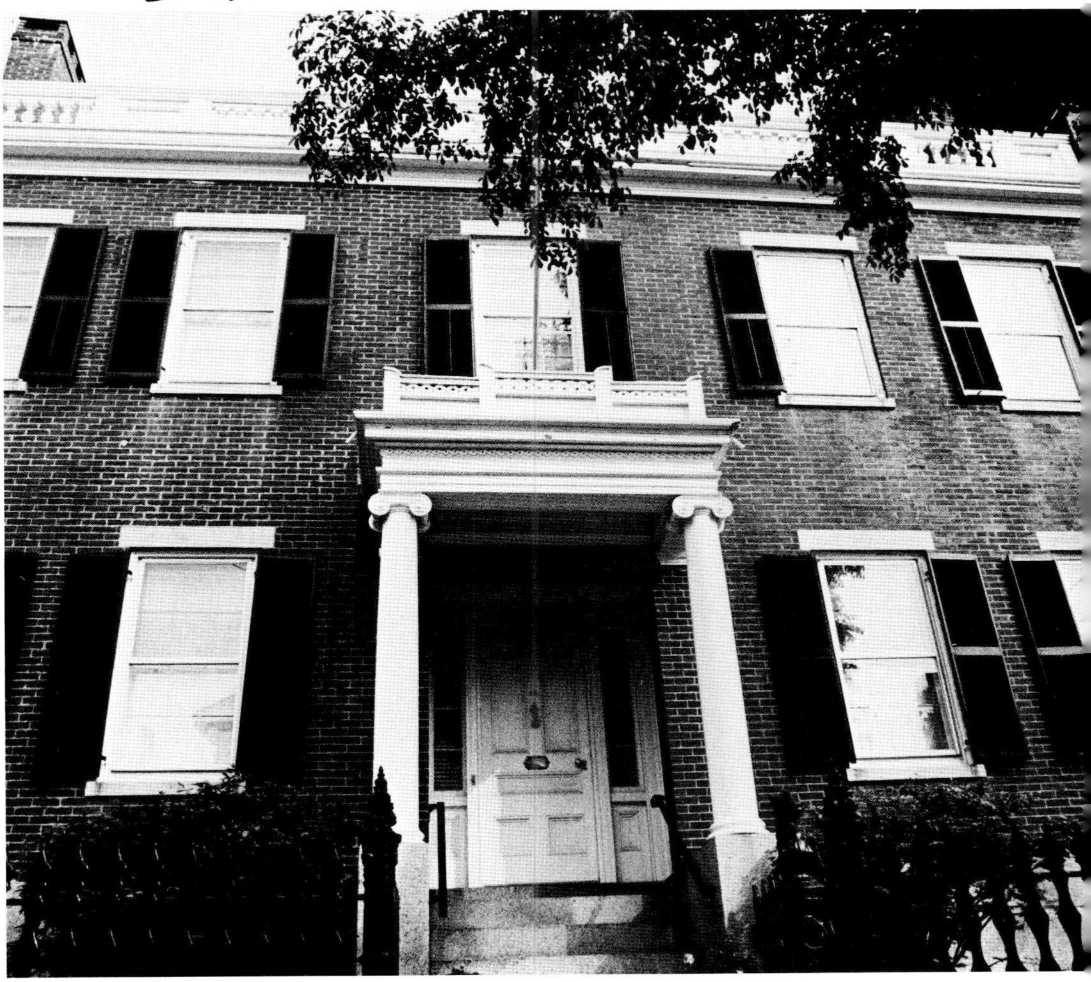

West Brick

93 Main Street

Maria Mitchell Birthplace

Vestal Street

Old Gaol (jail)

Built 1809

Old South Tower

Orange Street

Atheneum (library)

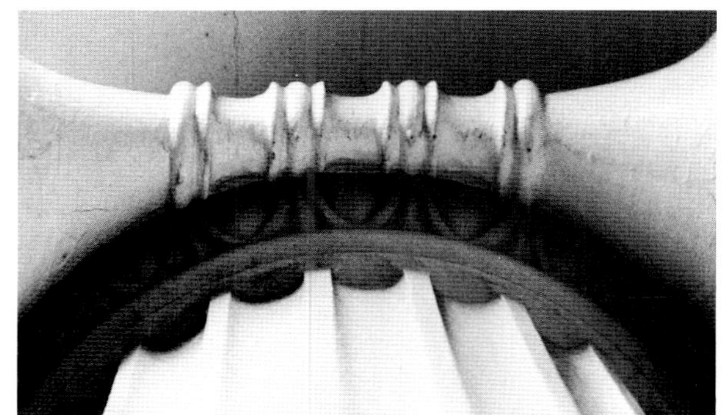

Lower India Street

The Pacific Club

Main Street

Built

1746

Built 1818

Main Street

Pacific National Bank

Built 1823

Methodist Church

Centre Street

Walnut Lane

Built 1723

Nathaniel Macy House

1800 House

Mill Street

Jethro Coffin House

Sunset Hill

The Oldest House

Built 1686

Congregational Church

96 Main Street
William Hadwen House

Nantucket Lightship Museum

Straight Wharf

Highest Point on Nantucket

Altar Rock

NANTUCKET: HISTORICAL SITES

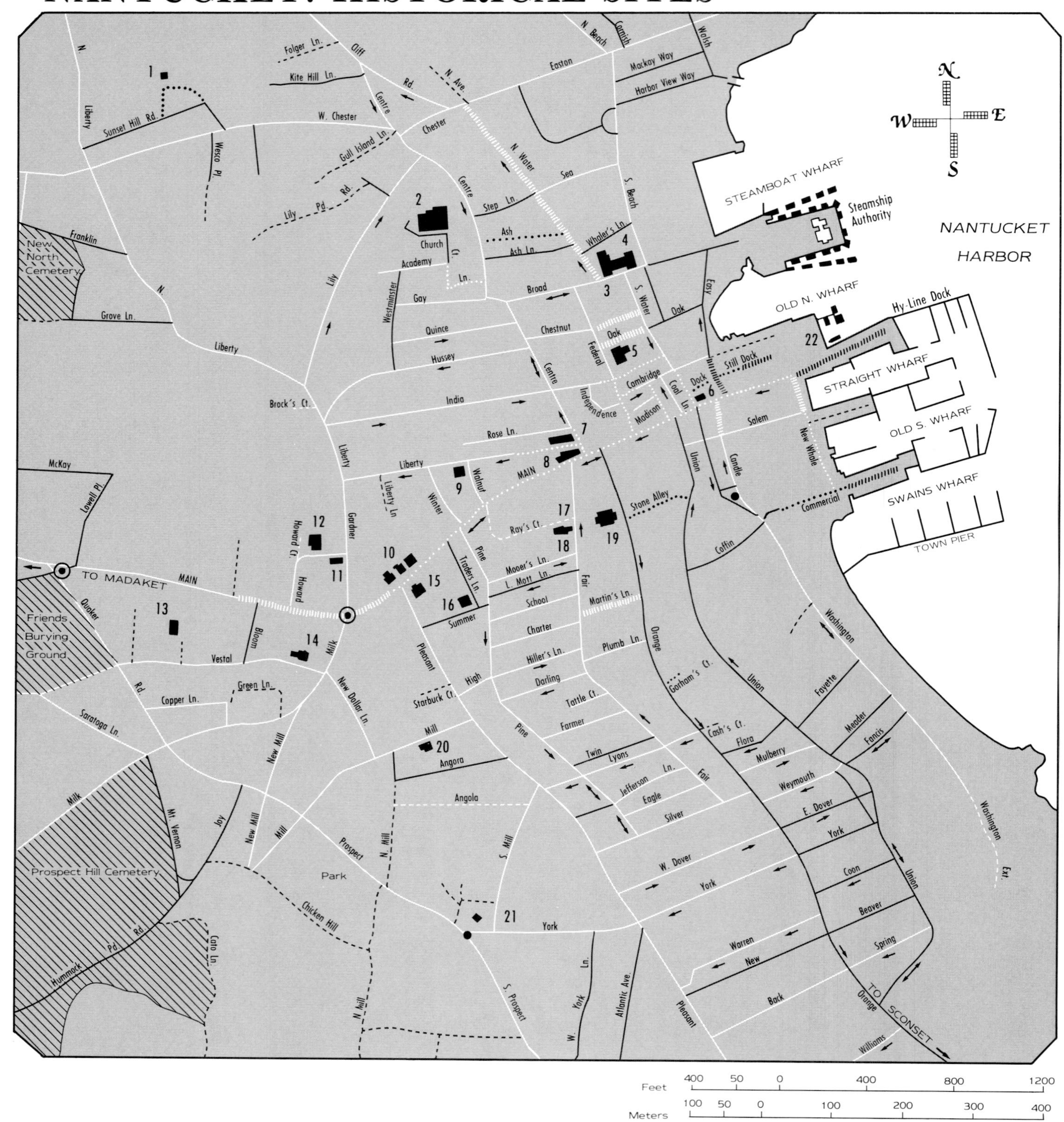

1. Oldest House
2. Congregational Church
3. Peter Foulger Museum
4. The Whaling Museum
5. The Atheneum
6. The Pacific Club
7. The Methodist Church
8. The Pacific National Bank
9. Nathaniel Macy House
10. The Three Bricks
11. Old Fire Horse Cart House
12. Greater Light Museum
13. The Old Gaol (Old Jail)
14. Maria Mitchell Birthplace
15. William Hadwen House
16. The Baptist Church
17. Fair Street Museum
18. Friends Meeting House
19. Old South Tower
20. 1800 House
21. The Old Mill
22. Nantucket Lightship Museum
23. Lifesaving Museum

HISTORICAL SITE: LIFE SAVING

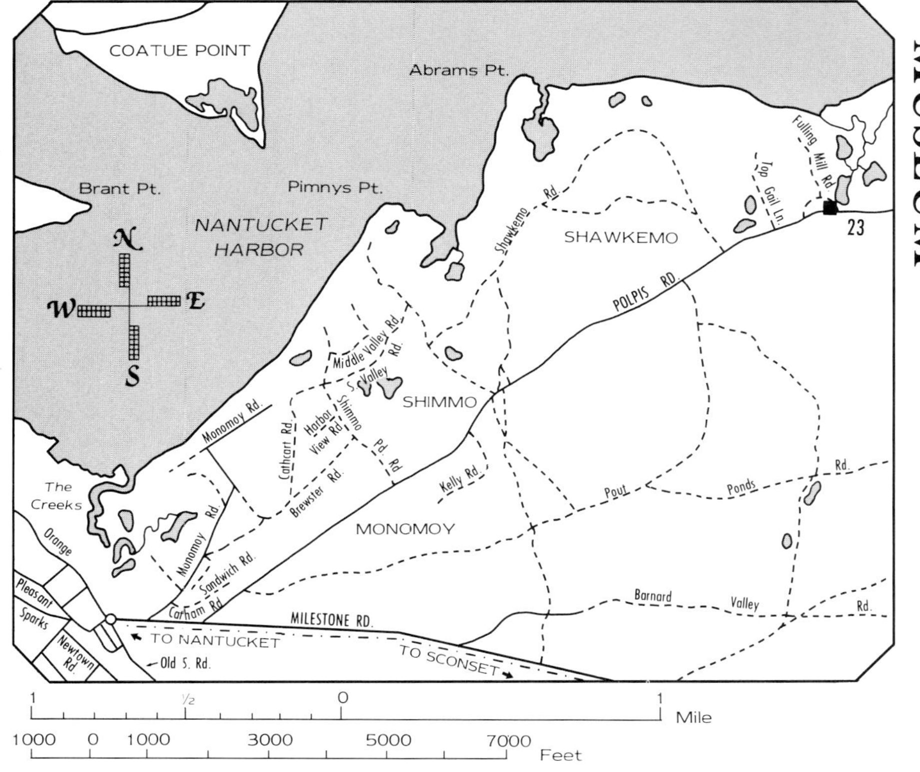

(White Roads) 1799 Roads: These roads are or follow what were the original 1799 roads.

———— Paved Roads

------- Unpaved Roads

·········· Cobblestone

⫻⫻⫻⫻⫻ Stone & Brick Roads

–·–·– Bike Path

→ One-way Roads

● Monument

○ Rotary

▨ Cemeteries

Outlying Areas

Section IV

Madaket

MADAKET: NANTUCKET

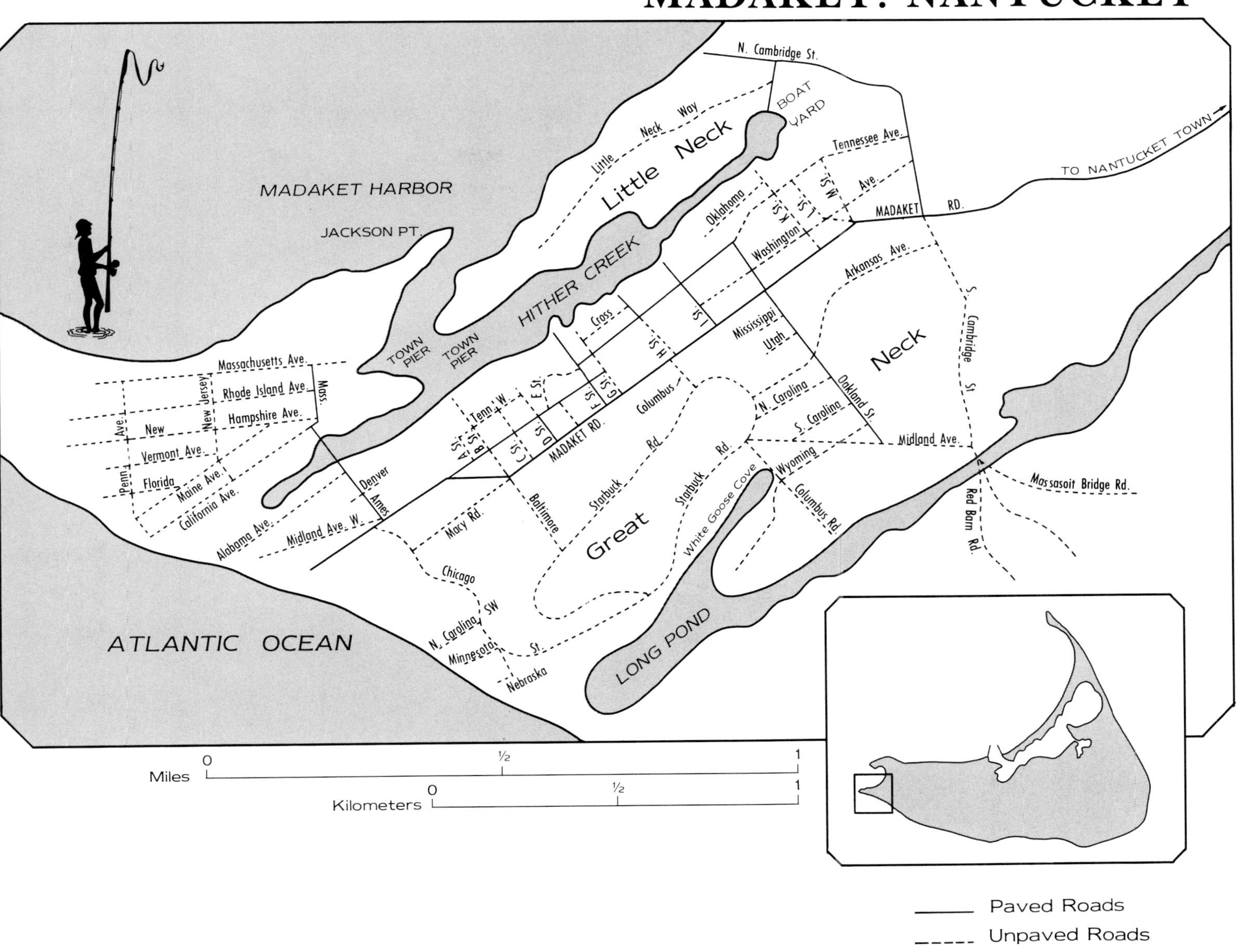

Eel Point

Cisco

Surfside

Monomoy

Quaise

Polpis

Wauwinet

Quidnet

Siasconset

Downtown, 'Sconset

Codfish Park, 'Sconset

'Sconset

The Town Pump

Built 1776

'Sconset

Auld Lang Syne

Moonlit Ocean, Codfish Park

'Sconset

North Bluff, 'Sconset

Sunrise

Sunset

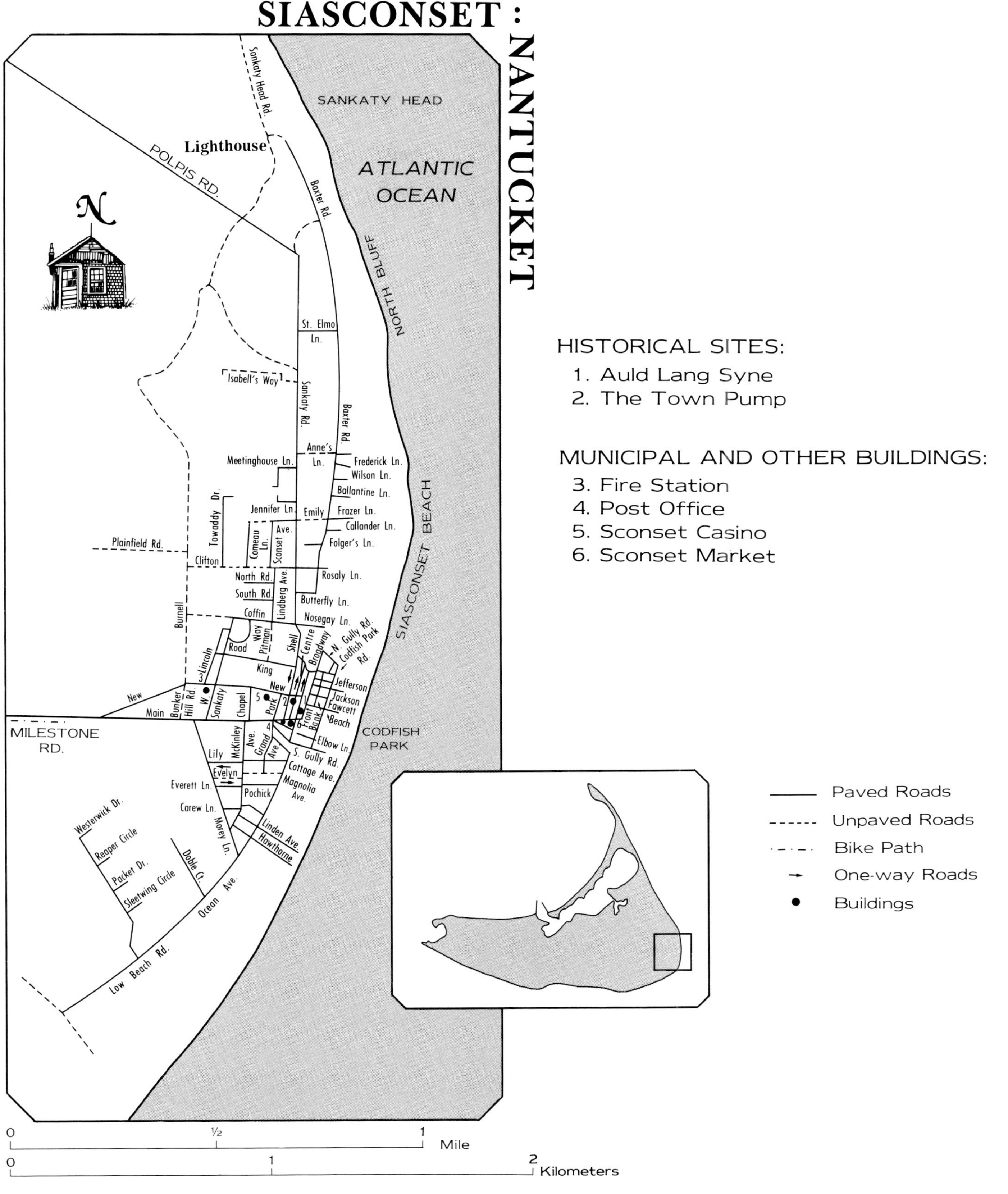

SIASCONSET : NANTUCKET
SANKATY HEAD
ATLANTIC OCEAN
Sankaty Head Rd.
POLPIS RD.
Lighthouse
N
NORTH BLUFF
Baxter Rd.
St. Elmo Ln.
Isabell's Way
Sankaty Rd.
Baxter Rd.
Anne's Ln.
Meetinghouse Ln.
Frederick Ln.
Wilson Ln.
Ballantine Ln.
Jennifer Ln.
Emily Ave.
Frazer Ln.
Callander Ln.
Folger's Ln.
Towaddy Dr.
Comeau Ln.
Sconset Ave.
Plainfield Rd.
Clifton
Rosaly Ln.
North Rd.
Lindberg Ave.
South Rd.
Butterfly Ln.
Burnell
Coffin
Nosegay Ln.
N. Gully Rd.
Codfish Park Rd.
Way
Pitman
Shell
Centre
Bragdway
Road
Lincoln
King
Jefferson
Jackson
Fawcett
New
Front
Bank
Beach
Bunker Hill Rd.
Sankaty
Chapel
Park
W
New
Main
Elbow Ln
SIASCONSET BEACH
CODFISH PARK
MILESTONE RD.
McKinley Ave.
Grand Ave.
Lily
S. Gully Rd.
Evelyn
Cottage Ave.
Everett Ln.
Pochick
Magnolia Ave.
Carew Ln.
Westerwick Dr.
Reaper Circle
Morey Ln.
Linden Ave.
Hawthorne
Packet Dr.
Doble Ct.
Sleetwing Circle
Ocean Ave.
Low Beach Rd.

HISTORICAL SITES:
1. Auld Lang Syne
2. The Town Pump

MUNICIPAL AND OTHER BUILDINGS:
3. Fire Station
4. Post Office
5. Sconset Casino
6. Sconset Market

Paved Roads
Unpaved Roads
Bike Path
One-way Roads
Buildings

0   ½   1   Mile
0   1   2   Kilometers

Ponds, Beaches & Lighthouses

Section V

Song Pond

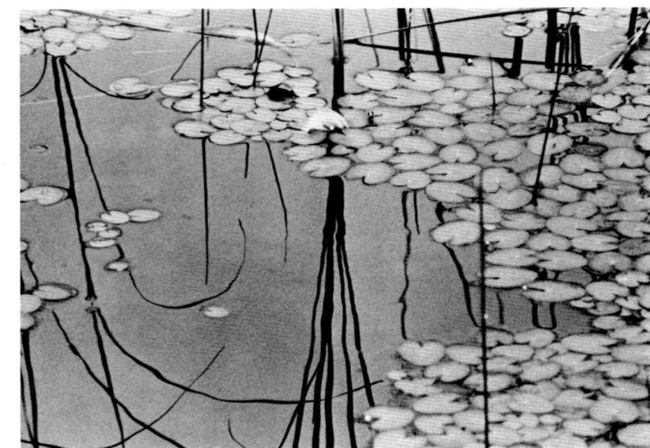

Washing Pond

North Head of Song Pond

Maxcy Pond

Capaum Pond

Middle Pond

Hummock Pond

Gibbs Pond

Head of Hummock Pond

Tom Nevers Pond

Miacomet Pond

Sesachacha Pond

Dionis Beach

Madaket Beach

Children's Beach

Siasconset Beach

Wauwinet Beach

Jetties Beach

Tom Nevers Beach

Cisco Beach

Surfside Beach

Coskata

end of Easton Street

Brant Point Lighthouse

Built 1902

End of Baxter Rd., Siasconset

Sankaty Head Lighthouse

Built 1826

Great Point Lighthouse

1818 — 1984

BEACHES   BEACHES   BEACHES

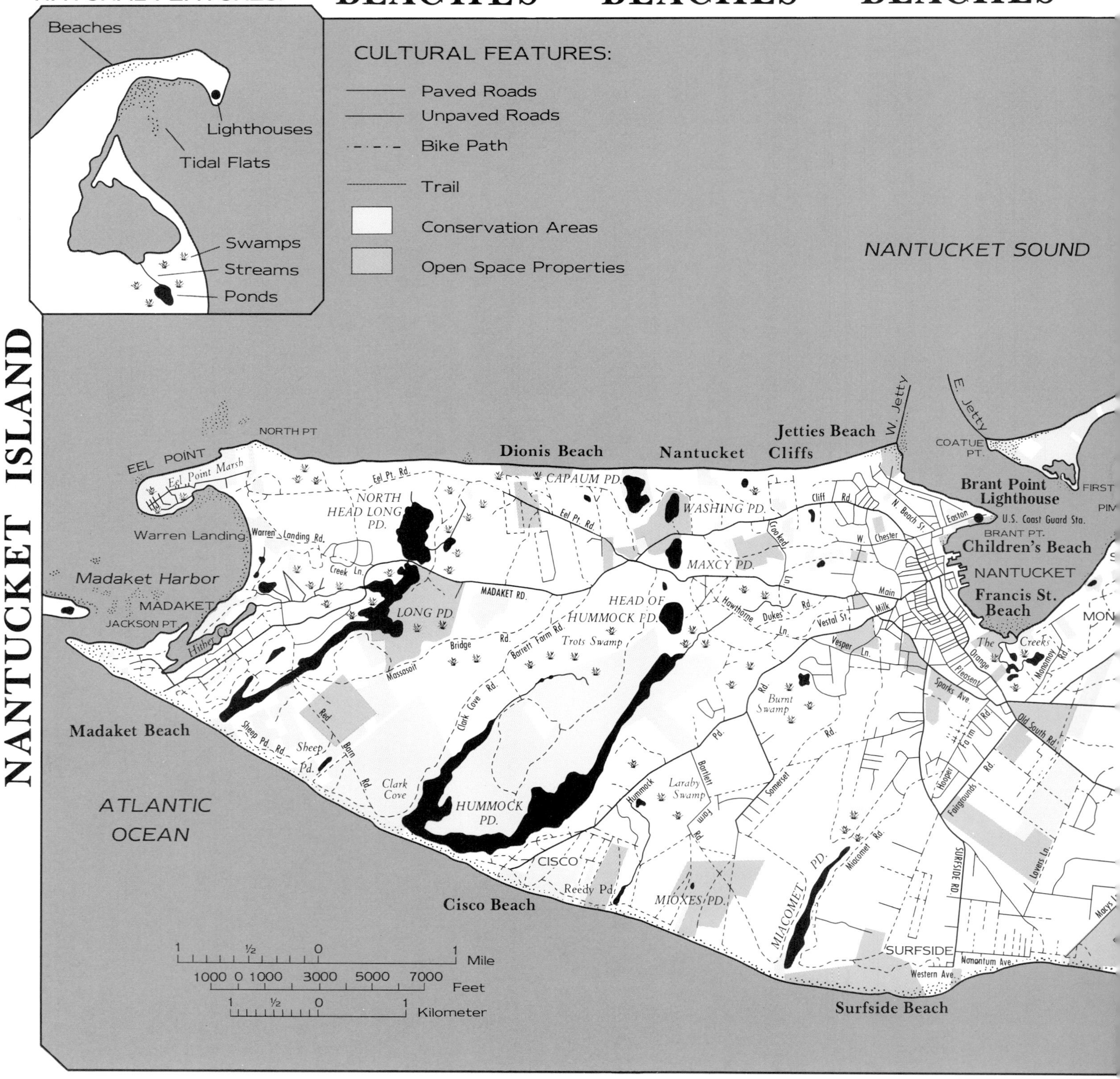

CULTURAL FEATURES:

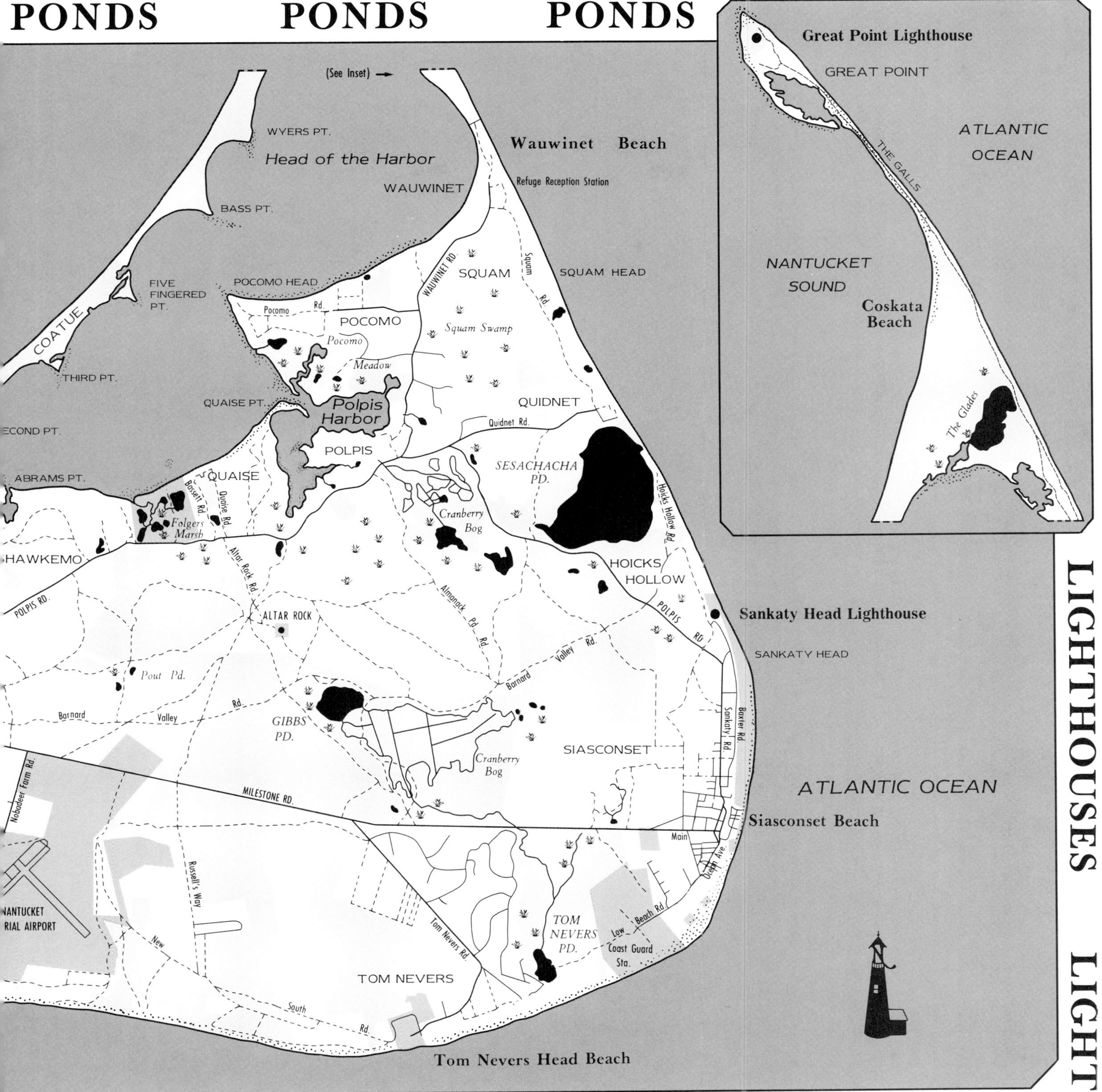

PONDS   PONDS   PONDS
Great Point Lighthouse
GREAT POINT
ATLANTIC OCEAN
THE GALLS
NANTUCKET SOUND
Coskata Beach
The Glades
(See Inset)
WYERS PT.
Head of the Harbor
Wauwinet Beach
WAUWINET
Refuge Reception Station
BASS PT.
POCOMO HEAD
SQUAM
Squam Rd.
SQUAM HEAD
WAUWINET RD.
FIVE FINGERED PT.
COATUE
Pocomo   Rd.
POCOMO
Squam Swamp
THIRD PT.
Pocomo
Meadow
QUAISE PT.
Polpis Harbor
QUIDNET
Quidnet Rd.
SECOND PT.
POLPIS
SESACHACHA PD.
ABRAMS PT.
QUAISE
Boxsett Rd.
Quaise Rd.
Cranberry Bog
Hoicks Hollow Rd.
Folgers Marsh
HAWKEMO
Altar Rock Rd.
HOICKS HOLLOW
POLPIS RD.
ALTAR ROCK
Almanack Pd. Rd.
POLPIS RD.
Sankaty Head Lighthouse
SANKATY HEAD
Pout Pd.
Valley   Rd.
Barnard
Sankaty Rd.
Barnard   Valley   Rd.
GIBBS PD.
Boxter Rd.
Cranberry Bog
SIASCONSET
ATLANTIC OCEAN
Milestone Rd.
Main
Siasconset Beach
Nobadeer Farm Rd.
Russell's Way
Ocean Ave.
NANTUCKET MEMORIAL AIRPORT
Tom Nevers Rd.
TOM NEVERS PD.
Low Beach Rd.
New
Coast Guard Sta.
TOM NEVERS
South   Rd.
Tom Nevers Head Beach
LIGHTHOUSES
LIGHT
LIGHTHOUSES
HOUSES

Leaving Nantucket...

Good-by my Nantucket, good-by Camelot . . .

make a wish...

throw twopence in...

Rounding the Fort...

Sweet Dreams Nantucket.

Acknowledgements

Thank you to all Nantucket establishment owners and managers for allowing photos to be taken and used in this book; to the Nantucket Historical Association for its generous help in providing photos of Great Point; to The Camera Shop on Nantucket for quick contact sheets; to Andrew Clements for his kind advice; many thanks to Ev Wingert and Jane Eckelman for their wonderful help and for making room 222 a part of my life; to Jeff Baker for all the 'running around' when I needed something sent from the mainland; to George G. for letting me put my paperwork all over his living room floor; to Roberta Holmberg for providing moral support; to my mother Ann, my Aunty Willa, and my cousin Mary for taking time from their vacation to do some extra fieldwork for the Maps; in memory of Greg Pineston who is always in my thoughts; to Evelyn and Stormy for always being full of life; and thanks to all at Heath Printers for their excellent work in printing 'Sweet Dreams'; thank you to Rebecca Brown for taking time away from her thesis to make maps for this book. A very special thanks to Nantucket Island, for without Nantucket as it is 'Sweet Dreams' would not have been possible. — T.S.

Many Thanks to Bob Campbell for his liaison work and Sally Sylvia in the Nantucket Superior Clerk Court Office for allowing access to their records. Thanks to Ernie Baclig for donating his car to the cause; and thanks to my parents for their encouragement and support. — R.B.

Map fieldwork and research — Rebecca Brown & Tom Simms. Map Design and Artwork — Rebecca Brown. Map design on pages 2 & 3 — Tom Simms, Artwork Rebecca Brown. Technical assistance — Jane Eckelman. Typesetting — Ernie Baclig. Lightship baskets in photos on pages 68 & 69 were made by Ann Simms, Willa Stiber, and Tom Simms.

Photos on page 120 were donated by the Nantucket Historical Association.